BE A SCIENTIST
INVESTIGATING
ELECTRICITY

JACQUI BAILEY

WAYLAND
www.waylandbooks.co.uk

First published in Great Britain in 2019 by Wayland
Copyright © Hodder & Stoughton, 2019
The text in this book was previously published
in the series 'Investigating Science'

Credits
Series Editor: Julia Bird
Illustrator: Ed Myer
Packaged by: Collaborate

HB ISBN 978 1 5263 1109 2
PB ISBN 978 1 5263 1110 8

Wayland
An imprint of
Hachette Children's Group
Part of Hodder & Stoughton
Carmelite House
50 Victoria Embankment
London EC4Y 0DZ

An Hachette UK Company
www.hachette.co.uk

Printed in China

MIX
Paper from
responsible sources
FSC® C104740
FSC
www.fsc.org

BE A SCIENTIST

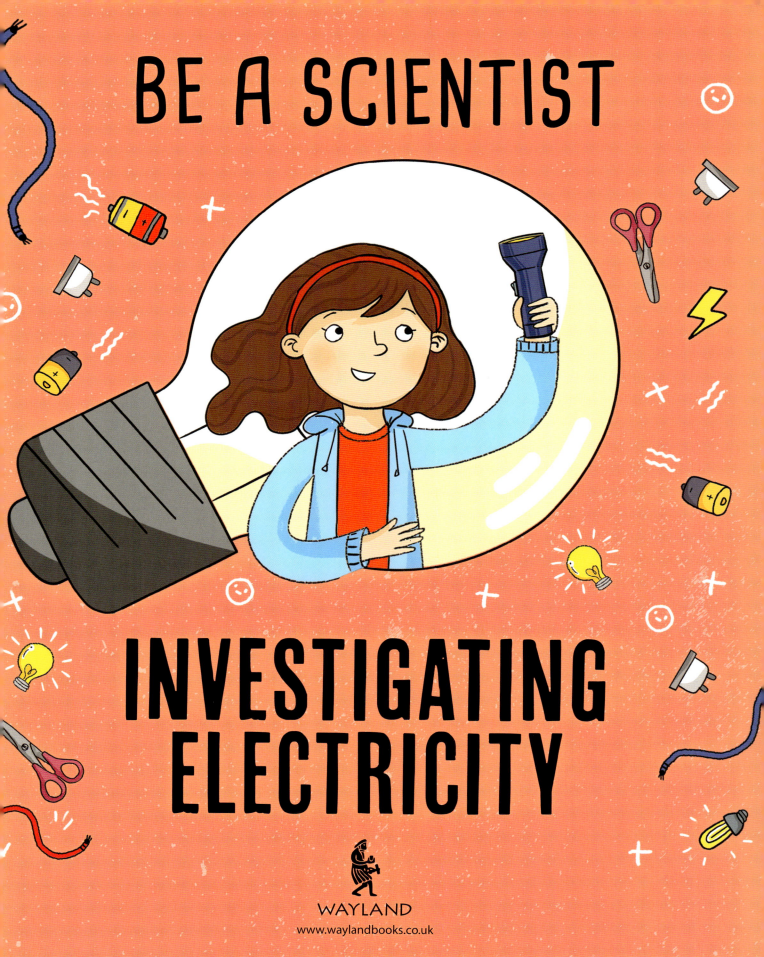

INVESTIGATING ELECTRICITY

WAYLAND

www.waylandbooks.co.uk

CONTENTS

WHAT IS ELECTRICITY?

Electricity is a type of energy. It makes all sorts of things work.

THINK about how most of the machines in your home work.

- You press a switch to turn on a ceiling light.
- You plug in the television to make it work.

How many things in your house are powered by electricity?

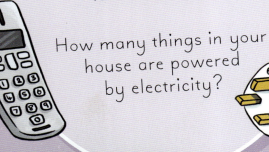

YOU WILL NEED
A sheet of lined paper
A pencil and a ruler

WHAT NEEDS ELECTRICITY TO MAKE IT WORK?

1 Draw a straight line down the middle of the piece of paper.

2 In the left-hand column, list all the things in your house that use electricity.

" BECAUSE...

We use electricity because it is a quick, handy source of energy. It is easily turned on and off so it can be used only when it is needed. "

LAMP
LAPTOP
RADIO

3 In the right-hand column, write down what each machine does. Ask an adult if you are not sure.

4 Group the machines on your list according to what they do. For example, do they give out light or heat, or sounds and pictures, or make something move?

HOW DO WE GET ELECTRICITY?

Most of the electricity we use comes from huge power stations. This type of electricity is called **mains electricity.**

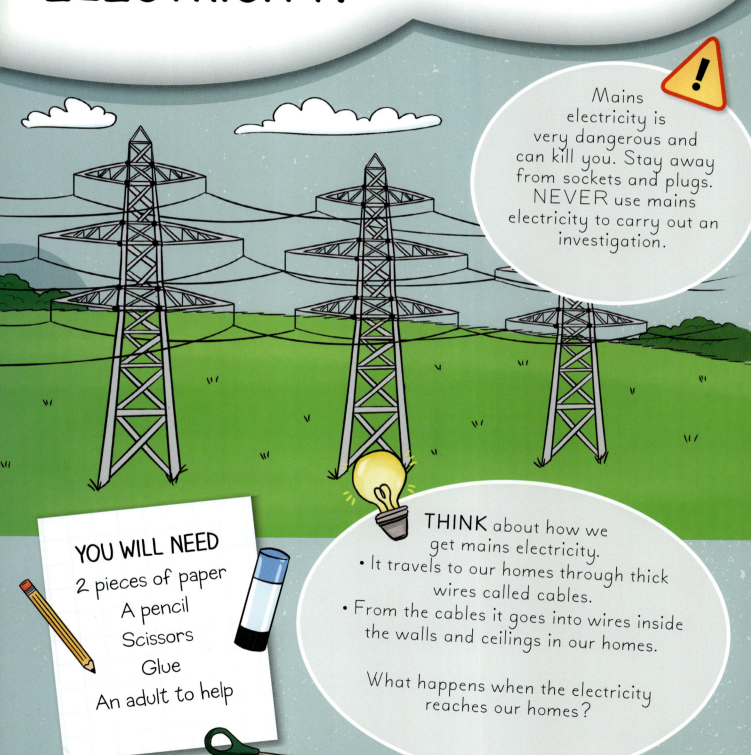

Mains electricity is very dangerous and can kill you. Stay away from sockets and plugs. NEVER use mains electricity to carry out an investigation.

YOU WILL NEED
2 pieces of paper
A pencil
Scissors
Glue
An adult to help

THINK about how we get mains electricity.
• It travels to our homes through thick wires called cables.
• From the cables it goes into wires inside the walls and ceilings in our homes.

What happens when the electricity reaches our homes?

HOW DOES ELECTRICITY WORK IN OUR HOMES?

1 Ask an adult to show you the following things, but do not touch them:
- An electricity meter
- A wall socket and switch
- A plug
- A table lamp or radio

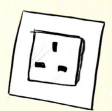

2 Make a small drawing of each one.

3 Cut out your drawings. Arrange them in the order in which you think they work to give us electricity. Now, glue them to the second piece of paper in this order.

" BECAUSE...

We need meters, sockets, switches and plugs because mains electricity is very powerful and these devices help to make it safe for us to use. "

9

PACKETS OF POWER

Batteries are small packets of electricity.

YOU WILL NEED
An alarm clock or stop watch
1 or 2 friends
Pencils and paper

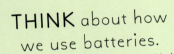

THINK about how we use batteries.

• Batteries fit inside all kinds of small machines, such as watches and mobile phones.

• Some machines that use batteries are portable – they can be carried about.

What machines can you think of that use batteries?

⚠ Batteries work using the chemicals they hold inside them. Batteries are safe to touch but DO NOT try to look inside one. The chemicals can burn you if they get on to your skin or clothes.

WHICH MACHINES USE BATTERIES?

1 Set the alarm clock or stop watch to ring in 5 minutes' time.

2 In that time, you and your friends each make a separate list of all the things you can think of that use batteries.

3 Compare your lists. Who has the longest list? How many different machines do you have altogether?

4 Look around the house. How many things that use batteries can you find?

" BECAUSE...

We use batteries because they are easy to carry around and safe to handle. Batteries do not give out any electrical energy until they are used with an electrical machine. "

RIGHT WAY, WRONG WAY

Batteries have to be put into the machines they power the right way around.

THINK about which way around batteries are put into machines.
- Mobile phones are designed so that the battery can only fit the right way around.
- Batteries in electric toys have to be put in correctly for the toy to work.

Which way around do batteries need to be?

YOU WILL NEED
A hand torch that you can take the batteries out of

HOW ARE BATTERIES USED?

1 Turn on the torch to make sure it is working.

2 Take out the torch's batteries. Look at them carefully. You should see a plus sign at one end of a battery. This is called the positive terminal. The other end is called the negative terminal. It should have a minus sign.

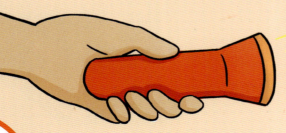

3 Put the batteries back in the torch so that the plus signs are facing each other. Screw the top back onto the torch and press the switch. Does it work?

4 Take the batteries out of the torch again. Put them in so that they are facing in the opposite direction to how you found them in step 2. What happens when you press the switch?

5 Now, put the batteries in as they were when you took them out in step 2. Which way do the batteries' plus and minus signs need to face to make the torch work?

"

BECAUSE...

The torch worked the third time because the batteries were the right way round. Batteries must be positioned properly in order for them to work. Many battery-operated devices have marks inside them to show which way the batteries should be placed.

"

GOING AROUND IN CIRCLES

For electricity to work, it has to flow in a loop called a **circuit**. An electrical circuit has different parts to it.

THINK about how a torch works.
- It has a light bulb, which needs electricity to light it up.
- It has batteries, which provide the electricity.
- It has a metal strip that links the bulb and batteries together so that electricity can flow between them.

This is a circuit. Can you make a circuit?

YOU WILL NEED

A helpful adult

Scissors

2 lengths of single-strand, plastic-coated wire

A small screwdriver

A bulb holder

A small torch bulb of 3 volts (3V) (see page 29 to find out about volts)

A C or AA size battery (1.5V)

Sticky tape

HOW DO CIRCUITS WORK?

1 Ask an adult to strip about 2 cm of the coating off both ends of the wires. Twist the ends of the wires to make them neat.

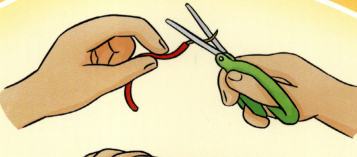

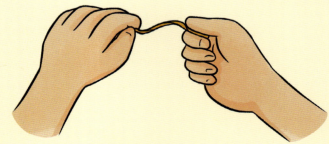

" BECAUSE...

The bulb lights up because electricity is flowing from the battery along the wire, through the bulb and back to the battery again in an unbroken circuit. **"**

3 Carefully screw the bulb into the bulb holder.

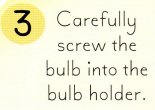

2 Use the screwdriver to loosen the two screws on either side of the bulb holder. Twist one bared end of each wire around the base of the screws. Tighten the screws again to hold the wires in place.

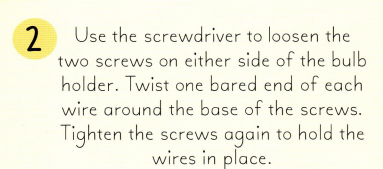

4 Tape the other ends of the wires to the positive and negative terminals of the battery. Make sure the bare wires are on the metal contact points of the battery. What happens to the light bulb?

WILL IT WORK?

If any part of a circuit is connected up wrongly, the circuit will not work.

YOU WILL NEED
A pencil and paper
The same circuit parts you used on pages 14–15

1 Look carefully at the following three circuits.

WHICH CIRCUITS WORK AND WHICH DO NOT?

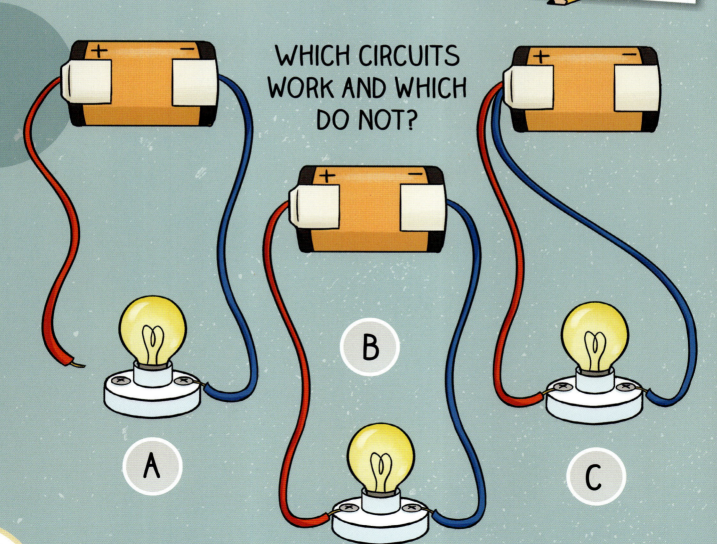

A

B

C

2 Write down which circuits you think will work and which will not.

3 Using the parts from the circuit you made on pages 14-15, make each of the circuits A, B and C in turn. Were you right or wrong?

BECAUSE...

Circuit A does not work because the circuit is not complete. There is a break in the circuit between the bulb and the wire. Circuit C does not work because both wires are connected to the same terminal on the battery. Electricity must flow from one end of the battery to the other. Circuit B works because electricity can flow from the battery to the bulb, and back to the other end of the battery - the circuit is complete.

ON AND OFF

Switches can turn a circuit on and off.

THINK about how you turn on electricity in your home.
- You flick a switch on a radio to turn it on or off.
- You press a switch on a computer to turn it on or off.

How do you think switches work?

YOU WILL NEED

The same circuit parts you used on pages 14–15 and 16–17

2 metal drawing pins

1 metal paperclip

A piece of balsa wood

An extra length of single-strand, plastic-coated wire

HOW DO SWITCHES WORK?

1 Connect up your circuit as on pages 14-15, but this time take one of the wires off the battery and wrap it securely around a drawing pin.

2 Push the drawing pin through the paperclip and into the balsa wood.

3 Connect the third piece of wire from the free end of the battery to the other drawing pin.

4 Push this pin into the wood (see left). Make the two drawing pins the same distance apart as the length of the paperclip.

5 What happens when the paperclip touches just one of the drawing pins? What happens when the paperclip touches both drawing pins?

BECAUSE...

When the paperclip touches just one drawing pin the light is off because there is a gap in the circuit. Electricity cannot flow if there is a gap in a circuit. When the paperclip touches both drawing pins, the gap is closed and electricity flows around the circuit. The paperclip acts as a switch. Switches open or close a gap in a circuit.

TEST YOUR SKILL

Simple circuits can be used in a lot of ways. Test your circuit-building skills by making an electronic game.

YOU WILL NEED
Sticky tack
A wooden board
A metal coat-hanger
Uncoated fuse wire
Tape and scissors
A 4.5V or 9V battery
A buzzer
3 lengths of wire
A small screwdriver

THINK about how each part of the circuit is linked together.

HOW STEADY IS YOUR HAND?

1 Put a lump of sticky tack onto the middle of the wooden board. Push the hook of the coat-hanger into it so that it stands upside down.

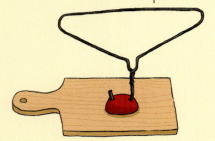

2 Loop the fuse wire through the coat-hanger and twist the ends into a handle, taping them up to hold it secure.

"BECAUSE...

When the loop touches the coat-hanger, the buzzer sounds because the loop acts like a switch. When the loop is not touching the coat-hanger there is a gap in the circuit and the buzzer does not make a noise. "

4 Twist the third wire from the battery to the top of the handle of the fuse wire loop. Add some tape to the bottom of the coat-hanger as a resting place for the loop. Can you move the loop around the coat-hanger without the buzzer sounding?

3 Connect one wire from the buzzer to the coat-hanger, and the second wire from the battery to the buzzer.

21

FLOWING ALONG

Electricity flows through some materials more easily than others. Materials that carry electricity well are called **conductors**. Those that do not are called **insulators**.

YOU WILL NEED

The same circuit parts you used on pages 18–19, but without the switch
Some test materials (e.g. some wood, a plastic ruler, paper, aluminium foil, a glass, a metal paperclip, an eraser)
A pencil and paper

THINK about the materials you use to make circuits.
• Wires carry the flow of electricity around a circuit.
• Wire is made of metal wrapped in plastic.

Which of the test materials are conductors and which are insulators?

WHICH MATERIALS MAKE GOOD CONDUCTORS?

1. Set up a circuit like the one on pages 18–19, but this time leave out the switch so that you have two loose ends of wire.

2 Touch the two ends of wire together to make sure your circuit is working properly.

3 Now touch the two ends to each of your test materials in turn.

4 Note down each material you use and whether or not the bulb lights up.

BECAUSE...

The bulb lights up with metal objects because metal is a good conductor. It does not light up when the circuit includes materials such as plastic and wood. These materials are good insulators. Why do you think electric wires are coated in plastic?

Material	Lights up?
eraser	no
glass	
pebble	
foil	

BRIGHTEN UP!

A circuit can have as many parts, or **components** attached to it as you like.

THINK about different types of circuit.

• Christmas tree lights are all part of one circuit. When the circuit is plugged in, all the lights come on at the same time.

What happens when you add parts to a circuit?

YOU WILL NEED

4 lengths of plastic-coated wire

A 1.5V battery

3 x 3V–4.5V bulbs and holders

Sticky tape

Scissors

A small screwdriver

A 9V battery

1 Build a circuit using two lengths of wire, a 1.5V battery and one bulb, as on pages 14-15.

2 Add another length of wire and another bulb to your circuit. What happens? Do both bulbs glow?

3 Replace the 1.5V battery with the 9V battery. Does this make a difference?

4 Add a fourth length of wire and a third bulb. What happens now? Are all the bulbs lit? Are they brighter or dimmer?

❝ BECAUSE...

When you add more bulbs to a low-**voltage** battery, the lights become dimmer. That's because each bulb gets a smaller share of the electricity. When you use a stronger battery, there is enough electricity for the bulbs to share between them and make them bright. But be warned, if the battery is too powerful, the bulbs will burn out and stop working. ❞

WILD ELECTRICITY

Electricity does not come only from power stations and batteries – it also exists naturally as **static electricity.**

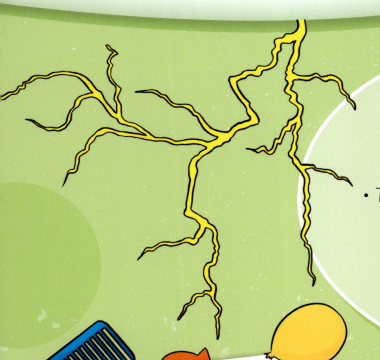

THINK about static electricity.
- **Lightning** is a really powerful flash of light and heat caused by static electricity.
- The crackles you might hear when you pull off a jumper are also made by static electricity.

What can you do with static electricity?

YOU WILL NEED
A blown-up balloon
A woolly sweater
Tissue paper cut into small shapes
Test materials (e.g. a wooden spoon, a plastic comb, aluminium foil)
Paper and a pencil

HOW CAN YOU MAKE STATIC ELECTRICITY?

1 Rub the balloon against the woolly sweater.

2 Hold the balloon against a wall and let go of it. What happens?

3 Rub the balloon again and hold it near the pieces of tissue paper. What happens to the paper?

4 Try rubbing some other materials on the sweater and hold them next to the pieces of tissue paper. Do any of them affect the paper? Make a record of those that do and those that do not.

BECAUSE...

The balloon and some of the other materials pull the tissue paper towards them because of static electricity. Rubbing things together makes a static electric charge build up on their surface. Depending on the material, this electric charge will either pull another material towards it or push it away.

USEFUL WORDS

Batteries

are like tiny portable power plants. They produce electricity by mixing together two chemicals. In some batteries, the chemicals are eventually used up and the batteries are then thrown away. There are other batteries that can be recharged and used again.

Circuits

are the paths that electricity flows around in order to make things work. Electricity must be able to flow in a complete loop from the power source (for example, a battery) around the circuit and back to the power source. If there is a break or gap in the circuit, electricity will not be able to flow.

Components

are the parts that make up a circuit. These are either the devices that need electricity to make them work, such as light bulbs, buzzers and motors, or they are the devices that control the flow of electricity, such as switches.

Conductors

are the materials that let electricity flow easily through them. Metals and water are good conductors.

Electricity

is a type of energy. We use it to give us light and heat and to power all sorts of machines. Electricity is just one form of energy. Our bodies use food energy to move around and grow, and cars use petrol energy to power their engines.

Insulators

are materials that slow down or stop the flow of electricity. Plastic and rubber are good insulators.

Lightning

is a giant spark of electricity that leaps between a cloud and the ground.

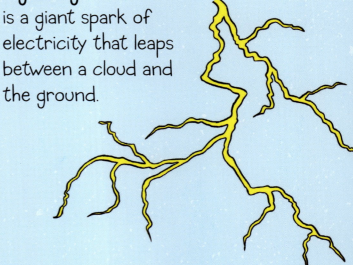

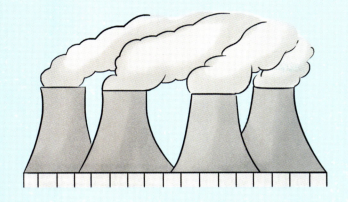

Mains electricity

is made in large power stations. Power stations use fuels, such as coal or gas, to make electricity. The electricity is then fed into thick wires, or cables, that carry it all over the country. Electricity travels blindingly fast. In fact, it travels at the speed of light – 300,000 kilometres per second.

Static electricity

is a form of electricity that exists naturally. It does not flow in a circuit, but builds up in materials when they rub together. If enough static electricity builds up, the electricity is forced to flow and jumps from one material to another as a spark.

Switches

are used to control the flow of electricity in a circuit. A switch turns a circuit off by opening up a gap in the circuit. Switches allow us to save electricity by using it only when we need to.

Voltage

is a way of measuring how strongly a battery or mains electricity pushes an electrical flow around a circuit. The strength of the push is measured in volts. A small battery may have 1.5V (1.5 volts) stamped on it. A stronger battery may have 9V. If more than one battery is used in a circuit, (for example, three 1.5V batteries) the number of volts adds up to a greater voltage (3 x 1.5 = 4.5 volts). Mains electricity is very powerful, it has a push of 240V.

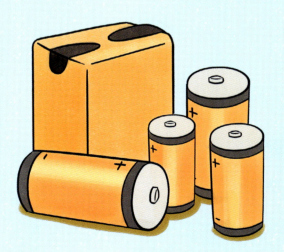

MORE INFORMATION

BOOKS TO READ

BOOM! Science: Electricity by Georgia Amson-Bradshaw (Wayland, 2018)
Horrible Science: Shocking Electricity by Nick Arnold (Scholastic, 2018)
Moving Up with Science by Peter Riley (Franklin Watts, 2016)

WEBSITES

Learn more about electricity, circuits, conductors and insulators at
www.bbc.com/bitesize/topics/zj44jxs

www.dkfindout.com/uk/science/electricity/ has lots of helpful information
on batteries, circuits and even electrical animals! It also includes an
electricity quiz.

PLACES TO VISIT

EDF Energy has eight visitor centres across the
UK which look at electricity in a fun and interactive way.
Visit www.edfenergy.com/energy/education/visitor-centres to find out more.

Visit the Science Museum in London to discover how electricity
has shaped our world.

NOTE TO PARENTS AND TEACHERS:

Every effort has been made by the publisher to ensure that these websites
contain no inappropriate or offensive material. However, because of the
nature of the Internet, it is impossible to guarantee that the content of
these sites will not be altered. We strongly advise that Internet access is
supervised by a responsible adult.

INDEX